A. L. SWAP
IN
THE CIVIL WAR

An oral history of his service as told to
Izora De Wolf

Edited by Ross E. Statham

Second Edition Copyright © 2022, Ross E. Statham

All rights reserved.

No part of this book may be reproduced, stored in a retrieval system, or transmitted by any means, electronic, mechanical, photocopying, recording, or otherwise, without written permission from the author.

ISBN: 978-1-7371314-4-1
ISBN (eBook): 979-8-9854044-0-1

Introductory Notes

This short and simple war story of my brother-in-law, Andrew La Fayette Swap, Civil War veteran and American patriot, was given to me, at my solicitation, during a brief visit at his home, near Albion, Pennsylvania in December of 1912, and is, in the main, told in his own words. It is my earnest hope that in these pages—got from the veteran's own lips—may be caught and held, for his children and the generations that shall come after them, some fugitive glimpse of the soldier-soul of the man whose part in the epic struggle of 1861-1865 is here so modestly narrated.

They—his children and grandchildren—will remember him as a silver haired man, bearing cheerfully and patiently the life-long burden of a physical ailment (asthma) brought home in 1866 from southern swamps and trenches; from blood-boiling forced marches and subsequent chilling upon the bare frozen ground, [and] from the hardships and privations innumerable that were the lot of the soldier in the Civil War.

I wish to show him, young, strong and ardent; brown of hair, blue of eye, and ruddy of cheek—a goodly offering upon the altar of Patriotism. I ask them to follow, with sympathy and understanding, through the scenes—sometimes sublime, sometimes tragic and sometimes—thank heaven! wholesomely and healingly ridiculous—through which these pages lead.

I trust that they may read into the story—between the lines—all the heroism and devotion that the modesty of the narrator so sedulously keeps in the background: and it shall be our abundant reward for a labor of love—his who told, and mine who transcribed these personal reminiscences of a stirring period of American history—if, at the end, they shall say: "This man was a representative Union Soldier; I am proud that he was my ancestor."

Izora De Wolf

Tell me the tale of your soldier days,
    Oh veteran tried and true:
Paint me the pageant through which you moved
    When you marched 'neath the Red, White and Blue.

What of the comrades, brave and young,
    Beside you in camp and field?
What of the falling flag upborne,
    And the righteous cause upheld?

What of the marches, deadly long?
    What of the hunger-throe?
What of the picket-watches lone,
    While the leaden night dragged slow?

What of the cold, and the cruel sun?
    What of the swamp and fen?
What of the fever's nightmare dream?
    What of the prison pen?

What of the hours of sick suspense
    By the camp fire's sullen glow;
As you waited the bugle call to arms
    Fronting the unseen foe?

Then what of the word of quick command,
    And the sudden battle lust?
The bloody struggle hand to hand?
    The smoke and the blinding dust?

Ah! What of the shouts of victory?
    The triumphant trumpet's blare?
What of the waving banners, gay
    And the blazing bonfire's glare?

Tell me the piteous glorious tale;
    Oh veteran tried and true;
Paint me the pageant, grim and grand,
    That your war-led steps passed through.

Second Edition Introduction

My wife's family has, in their possession, an ancient copy of "the book" (as they call it)- of which they are justifiably proud. I wanted this great little book to receive a fuller audience.

The book was transcribed from interviews with Andrew La Fayette Swap fifty years after the events (1912) by his sister-in-law Izora De Wolf. I sought as much as possible to leave his original statements intact.

De Wolf did a superb job in transcribing his story. However, she inserted comments within her original transcription which were her own musings and (in my opinion) detracted from his story; I removed most of them. If my doing so annoys you, please forgive me.

Regarding any inaccuracies the reader may discover, the errors are purely my own.

Ross Statham, Chipley, Florida
November 2021

Second Edition Dedication

This book is dedicated to the 618,222 men who died during the 1861-1865 American Civil War—men from both sides who fought for what they believed. This loss of life represented about 2% of the population of the north and south at the time. In 2021 terms the equivalent loss would be over six *million* American soldiers lost within a four-year period, through combat or disease. How would we feel about losing six million soldiers today?

Among the dead was my grandmother's grandfather—killed in action April 15, 1864 in the Alabama infantry. He was the grandfather she never knew.

This edition is dedicated to each of these men who died— and to the parents, wives, brothers, sisters and especially the children they left behind.

A special thanks to my wife Audrey Ring Statham, and to Ron and Beverly Ring, who shared "The Book" with the "Johnny Reb" who married into the family. They have gone out of their way to demonstrate that I'm a loved, appreciated (and occasionally tolerated!) part of the Ring and Swap extended families. And in the process, I've discovered that Yankees aren't nearly as bad as I was originally led to believe!

Ross E. Statham
Chipley, Florida- November 2021

Table of Contents

The Volunteer—Fever 3

In The Color Guard—Engagement
    At Springfield 9

Battle of Pea Ridge—Fighting
    Guerillas—Camp Life 13

Promotion—Dealing With Guerillas 19

Newtonia—Marching, Skirmishing, etc. 23

Battle of Prairie Grove—Disciplined—
    On to Cape Girardeau 27

Girardeu—The Little Drummer 33

Battle of Chalk Bluff 35

Siege of Vicksburg—Yazoo City 37

In Louisiana—Morganza Bend—On to
    Rio Grande—Chumming with
    the Mexicans 41

Fun in Camp—Free State Festivities 47

Photo of Swap's fiancé, Loretta De Wolf 51

Furlough—Forgotten Etiquette— 　　Back South	53
Siege and Assault of Blakely, Alabama— 　　Lee's Surrender—Hunting Alligators— 　　Another Furlough	59
Mustered Out—Final Tragedies—Wedding Bells	67
Principal Battles and Skirmishes in which the 　　Thirty-Seventh Illinois Infantry Took Part	71
Izora De Wolf Poetry	73
About the Second Edition Editor	91

A. L. SWAP IN THE CIVIL WAR

An oral history of his service as told to Izora De Wolf

Second Edition by Ross E. Statham

ANDREW LA FAYETTE SWAP
In 1864, Sergeant's Uniform

The Volunteer—Fever

I was born at "Porkey Street," Erie County, Pennsylvania, near Cherry Hill, on October 6, 1841, and lived with my uncle, Jacob Swap, between the ages of four and seventeen. I then went to La Salle County, Illinois, to rejoin my parents, Andrew and Sibyl Hitchcock Swap, who had gone west some years earlier. Here I worked at various jobs for at time; then, for two years, on a farm for Albert J. Goodspeed, a Methodist preacher and ardent abolitionist. Goodspeed was a conductor on the "Underground Railroad" and assisted runaway slaves.

On the 17th of April 1861, five days after Sumter was fired upon[1], I went out to drag [the field], but, instead, hitched the horses to the wagon wheel, left the drag in the field, and went to tell Goodspeed that I was going to enlist. I enlisted at Ottawa, Illinois for three months[2],

---

[1] History records that many young men in the northern states were ambivalent towards the succession—until the American flag was fired upon at Ft. Sumter. Three days later, Lincoln called for 75,000 volunteers, including from the "holdout" states—Virginia, North Carolina, Tennessee, and Arkansas. They would not provide these volunteers, instead voting to join the Confederacy.

[2] Both sides were convinced that it was going to be a short war. His three months was a typical enlistment period.

in Company I, 11th Illinois Infantry; and was mustered into the United States service as a private on April 19th [1861]. My height was recorded as 5 feet 10½ inches. We were transported by rail to Villa Ridge, Illinois, north of Cairo, where we drilled and learned soldiering for about four weeks.

I then took typhoid fever and was sent to the hospital, where my brother, Bert, came and nursed me. After the fever turned the surgeon said that I would die and must be removed from the hospital, as a death there would have a bad effect on the other sick men. Bert got me a place in a private house—that of a man named Wood. Altogether, I lay six weeks delirious. While convalescing I wanted a blackberry pie and received and ate a quarter section.

When I was able to be moved, Captain William Gibson, having already done all in his power for me during my illness, got transportation for Bert and me to go home.[3] He had previously telegraphed my people of our arrival. Mr. Goodspeed had especially requested Captain Gibson, a brother mason, to do for me all that he would do for himself (Goodspeed.) When I became able to drive a team to Ottawa, I weighed 126 pounds, my normal weight being about 180. I think I probably weighed not more than a hundred pounds when the fever turned.

---

[3] He was either discharged or placed on medical furlough due to the extremely serious nature of this illness.

The Volunteer—Fever

On August 20, 1861, I enlisted at Mendota, Illinois, in Company E, 37th Illinois Infantry[4], "for three years or during the war," rendezvous being at Camp Webb, Chicago, and was mustered into the United States service as corporal on September 18, 1861.

Out first march was from Camp Webb to the [Chicago] Board of Trade, where we were presented with a stand of colors. A regimental flag and banner were presented by the Board of Trade, of which Julius White was a member. We took train on the same day, September 19, for St. Louis. The train stopped and a number of the boys jumped off to get peaches, and had not time to board the train again before it started; but so many of the boys on board put on the brakes[5], that the train had to stop for them. We ferried across the river from Illinois Town (East St. Louis) on the 20th, marched to the headquarters of the Department Commander, General Fremont[6], and were reviewed by him and his staff. (I could not double quick for a year because of typhoid weakness.) At

---

[4] The 37th Illinois was formed in Chicago on September 18, 1861 and disbanded May 15, 1866. Andrew Swap was a member of the regiment its entire lifetime.

[5] This was done by pulling on a signaling cord in the passenger car.

[6] Major General John C. Frémont (1813-1890) was an explorer of the American west in three expeditions in the 1840's. In August 1861 he ordered the confiscation of the property of Missourians in rebellion as well as the state's slaves. He was relived of his command for insubordination by Abraham Lincoln.

this review, Fremont's wife, Jessie[7], tied a bunch of red, white and blue ribbons on our flag staff, and our banner bore Fremont's portrait.

We next marched to Benton barracks[8], where we remained, drilling, etc., for one week, and then took steamer to Booneville, Missouri, stopping at Jefferson City enroute.

After staying in Booneville about a week, we drew baggage teams—unbroken mules, which had to be lassoed and dragged to a wagon on which a man stood and dropped the harness on to them.

While encamped at Booneville, I stood my first picket guard. Reserve post was near Booneville. Being corporal of guard, I had to post the guard. I had a fire built in a ditch and a board laid over it to conceal it. I lay down on the board and went to sleep, rolled off into the fire and burnt my overcoat.

We started with our raw baggage teams on a march to Springfield, Missouri. The first day's march from Booneville was the hardest I ever experienced. We were green and unseasoned and loaded like "Cy Clegg[9]," and only covered seven miles. On the third day we arrived

---

[7] Jessie Benton Frémont was quite popular with the American public. She was the daughter of Senator Thomas Hart Benton; she and her father introduced Frémont to the Washington elite and was instrumental in his rise to prominence.

[8] Located at what is today's St. Louis Fairground Park.

[9] Clegg was an early silent American film actor. The reference is unclear, but refers to some humorous role Clegg played in one of his films. It would appear to be a popular culture reference.

near Otterville, Missouri, and camped in the mud. Here I had my first foraging experience. Skirmishing around with A. W. Edwards we found some pigs in the brush just right for roasting. Edwards shot at them repeatedly with his revolver, but missed and we did not have pork for supper.

Next day we moved on to Otterville Prairie, where we remained for several days drilling. Here the first death in our company occurred, and the dead comrade was buried with military honors. Our chaplain here preached his first and last sermon. The men would not listen to him unless compelled, because he was a gambler, etc. The captain of our company was P. B. Rust.

Continuing our march to Springfield, we reached Warsaw, Missouri, where the company went on a forced march [back] to Springfield, Missouri. On this day's march the only ration was one hard tack issued to each front-rank man. He broke it in two, and gave half to the rear man. We brought good appetites with us into Springfield.

On the afternoon of this march, we met General Frémont returning to St. Louis. He had been superseded by General Hunter[10], his idea of marching south from Springfield, the point of concentration, freeing slaves and living off the country being too radical for the government[11]. As Frémont passed, the regiment standing at

---

[10] Lincoln had replaced Frémont with General David "Black Dave" Hunter (1802-1886) who had a relatively short and uneventful tenure as commander before being promoted and sent East.

[11] As noted earlier, Frémont had been relieved of his command.

attention, a high wind caught the regimental banner and tore it through his portrait.

After a few day's rest we marched back to Lamine River[12], and went into Winter quarters. Here we drew our first pay for three years' service. We were paid in greenbacks at the rate of $11.00 a month[13], worth less than $5.00 in gold and silver. One soldier, I remember, looked at his money and called it "damned shinplasters."

During December [1861] we marched to Georgetown, Missouri to intercept the retreat of a rebel recruiting camp at Lexington, Missouri, and captured it. The march back to Lamine River was made through a foot of snow—heavy marching and no roads. Arrived at Lamine River, having no shovels, we kicked away the snow and set up tents. Comrade Robert Ashley, though sick with measles, had been obliged to march, and warm and tired as he was, was without cover till this was done. I carried straw half a mile to make him a "nest" and covered him with blankets. Other soldier's blankets froze to the ground that night. Next day we cut wood for fires. We were ordered to build chimneys to tents, and the Colonel offered $5.00 as a prize for the best chimney.

---

[12] The Lamine is a tributary of the Missouri River.

[13] $11 in 1861 is worth about $366.56 in 2021 dollars.

In The Color Guard—Engagement At Springfield

We had a fairly comfortable winter till about February 1st [1862], when we were again ordered to Springfield under General Curtis14. We marched through Syracuse and camped at Tipton, where we had a fall of snow. Next morning, we took up our line of march for Lynn Creek, Missouri, and ferried across [the] Osage River. This took two days. We then marched to Lebanon, Missouri where we stayed two days and had division drill. I had to fall out on account of weakness. Captain Rust had annexed a negro on this march, who wished to go with the regiment. His master learned of this and came to Lebanon in search of his slave. The captain being warned, sent two men with the negro and had them march parallel with the regiment, but not too near it, while the slave owner hunted up and down the line for his human property.

The death of First Sergeant Thomas Newell having left a vacancy in office, the captain appointed one of the

---

[14] Brigadier General Samuel Ryan Curtis (1805-1866) replaced Hunter on December 25, 1861. He is noted for his victories at Pea Ridge (1862) and Westport (1864).

two men who had guarded the negro to the vacancy, as a reward for this service. McCord, the man appointed, was in the color guard, and a vacancy here was thus created. Sergeant Manning searching for a man to fill this vacancy in the color guard, picked me for this service.

The guard was composed of eight corporals. Their duty was to go with and guard the colors whenever sent out—they and a sergeant who carried the colors making a square of nine. They had no other duties and were forbidden to fire their guns unless the colors were directly attacked; holding their fire to protect the colors, especially in case of an attempt to "rush" and capture them.

On the morning when the regiment was to resume its march to Lebanon, comrade and tentmate Lane was found dead in the tent, and two comrades stayed behind to bury him. In about a week we came within seven miles of Springfield and ran on to a rebel picket line. We then had the usual picket firing, cannonading, etc., till we reached Springfield. The rebels, few in number, left Springfield with little resistance and Curtis' army took possession, Curtis now being in command. After two days we took up the pursuit and chased the rebels for about a week—overtaking them each night and skirmishing with the rear guard. Pursued and pursuers had then reached Arkansas.

Having outstripped our baggage train, we now camped for four days near Cross Hollow—deep ravines in the form of a cross. During these four days we lived on what little we could find, and on raw corn, which we ground in our coffee mills, sometimes parching it before grinding. Our baggage train having come up we moved camp back Pea Ridge and remained there, encamped on Sugar Creek, till March 6, 1862.

Seigel's division encamped ten miles below at Bentonville, was attacked on this day, March 6th, and driven back to Pea Ridge. Expecting attack on the night of the 6th, General Curtis threw up barricades, etc., but the enemy, instead of attacking Curtis on Sugar Creek, took the road farther west which led to Curtis' rear.

Battle of Pea Ridge—Fighting Guerillas—Camp Life

In the morning, March 7 [1862], finding the enemy squarely in his rear, Curtis had to change front and defend his position. During the forenoon the division to which I belonged—Curtis' left wing, commanded by Jeff C. Davis15—was moved to the left.

At Lee Town we threw off and piled our knapsacks. These knapsacks were taken for the use of the wounded, excepting mine, which was returned to me by a friend who stood guard over them. After leaving Lee Town we went about eighty rods[16] west and marched to right flank in line of battle in the timber. Here we ran on to the Johnnies lying in the brush and engaged them, but were greatly outnumbered and fell back. We re-formed and again advanced, met the same resistance and again fell back. This happened three times, our division

---

[15] Brigadier General Jefferson Columbus Davis (1828-1879) was a "regular" US Army officer, and known for having a name highly similar to the President of the Confederacy. He was in the garrison at Ft. Sumter in April 1861.

[16] One "rod" equals 16.5 feet. 80 rods is one-quarter of a mile.

being opposed by McCullough's and McIntosh's entire commands.

Major J. C. Black now rode up to Manning, our color bearer and rebuked him for falling back; though only three or four of the color guard now remained alive and unhurt. The regiment now advanced for the fourth time. Manning, feeling himself unjustly censured, marched the color guard consisting now of only three men, about two rods[17] in advance. We knelt down so that the regiment could fire over our heads: and Manning, kneeling on his left knee, and holding his flag staff in his left hand drew his revolver with his right (contrary to his orders) and proceeded to attempt to annihilate the Southern Confederacy. A bullet cut off his left forefinger, and simultaneously one struck him in the breast. Perhaps the same bullet may have inflicted both wounds. I heard the thud of the bullet; Manning fell on his face—dead, as I supposed—I caught the falling flag, passed it to Conover, and thereafter guarded it while Conover carried it.

I was astonished after the battle to meet Manning alive and well. He had been struck by a spent ball.

The command being obliged to retreat behind its battery, the latter was captured by the enemy. One man straddled a gun and hurrahed for Jeff Davis. He was immediately struck by a bullet and killed. *(I could not induce Sergeant Swap to state more definite whether the*

---

[17] About 33 feet.

BATTLE OF PEA RIDGE—FIGHTING GUERILLAS—CAMP LIFE

bullet came from the ranks of the grey or those of the blue.—I. De W.) [18]

Reinforcements arriving, the battery was re-captured, and the enemy forced retreat, being driven half a mile completely off the field. We held our position till midnight, when we were ordered to Curtis' extreme right.

At daybreak on the 8th our brigade was ordered out in front of Elkhorn tavern to draw the enemy's fire and ascertain his position, which we did—promptly. The enemy's masked batteries opened fire upon us and an artillery duel ensued. We presently silenced the enemy's guns, firing till we received no response. Our brigade moved farther to the right, and our whole army advanced and drove the enemy from his position, ending the fight.

This was a three days' battle, including Siegel's engagement at Bentonville, in which we did not take part. Our immediate command was engaged for two days only.

At such times I had no realization of the flight of time. Going into the battle in the morning, night was upon us before I thought of expecting it.

Having captured our supply trains, the enemy lived upon our supplies during this battle of Pea Ridge. We found partly used sacks of our flour by their abandoned fires—also our mail sacks. A letter from my brother-in-law, Edmund P. Dodge, which had contained a dollar's worth of stamps was found, minus the stamps. As we were unable to obtain stamps here, this was aggravating.

---

[18] The man straddling the cannon was a Confederate. Union reinforcements arrived and the gun was re-captured.

Our regiment, of about 450 men, lost 145 men, killed and wounded at Pea Ridge, and our company of about 45[19] lost 17.

The Confederate forces here numbered some 25,000, commanded by Generals Price and Van Dorn[20]. The Federal forces aggregated about 13,000, commanded by General Samuel R. Curtis.

This was the only general engagement in which the Confederates used Indian troops. They had here about five hundred, commanded by General Albert Pike[21]. Their part of the battle consisted—characteristically—chiefly in killing the wounded and scalping the dead after the engagement[22].

(Sergeant Swap told the following incident sheepishly, yet with evident enjoyment of the joke, though it was on himself.—I. De W.)

---

[19] A full-strength company had 100 men.

[20] Major General Sterling Price (1809-1867), and Major General Earl Van Dorn (1820-1863). Van Dorn was senior and was in command.

[21] According to the Oklahoma Historical Society, there were "almost 900" (not 500) of the Cherokee 1st and 2nd Mounted Rifles in the Confederate Army from the Indian Territory (modern Oklahoma) present at the battle, who (by treaty) were not to be used outside of the Indian Territory.

[22] Their role was to help Van Dorn's calvary attack and subdue a Union (Iowa) battery on March 7th, but it is recorded that things got out of hand. There were confirmed killings of wounded Union soldiers, and at least eight Union dead (or wounded) were scalped. It was a major source of embarrassment for General Pike and the Confederacy.

Battle of Pea Ridge—Fighting Guerillas—Camp Life

During this battle was the only time I ever got scared and ran. After drawing the enemy's fire at Elkhorn Tavern, our company was deployed as skirmishers and was sent out in front of the regiment. Not expecting an immediate attack, the boys were gossiping and laughing, when a volley of cannister swept screaming over our heads. It came so suddenly that my heels ran away with my head, and I ran so fast a cannon ball would not have caught me. After a rod or two my scattered wits returned to me, and I made as much haste to return to my position as I had to leave it. Nobody, apparently, had noticed my little trip on French leave.

We stayed at Pea Ridge for three days, burying our dead and caring for our wounded. On the first day after the battle a Confederate officer with escort appeared, carrying a flag of truce, and asked permission to bury the Confederate dead, but did not bury nearly all of them. On the same day the woods caught fire and burned many of the dead beyond recognition. Probably some wounded were burned also. Our first lieutenant was wounded here, and died on the second day after. He was buried on the field. In his death the service lost a fine officer.

Promotion—Dealing With Guerillas

We now broke camp, marched three miles down Sugar Creek and made a new camp to escape the stench of the battlefield.

On March 9 [1862] I was appointed sergeant; a vacancy having been caused by the death of the lieutenant and the promotion of other sergeants. This took me out of the color guard and put me back on duty with the company.

In a few days we broke camp on Sugar Creek and marched leisurely back toward our base of supplies at Springfield. Arriving at Cassville, Missouri, General Curtis, with all his army except the 37th Illinois, one battalion of the 1st Missouri Cavalry and one section of the 2nd Illinois Light Artillery, marched to Helena, Arkansas on the Mississippi River. We were thus detached at Cassville and never rejoined Curtis' command.

At about that time our colonel, Julius White[23], was promoted to Brigadier General and transferred to the Eastern Department [of the Union Army]. In his farewell address he gave the regiment credit for his promotion

---

[23] Brigadier General Julius White (1816-1890) was a former businessman who later served as the Ambassador to Argentina.

which, he said, was the result of the gallant conduct of the enlisted men.

We remained at Cassville till July 1 [1862], scouting, drilling, and fighting the guerillas, with which region was infested. While at Cassville, our company went to Keetsville for three weeks. Here my bunk-mate and I went out after some milk or buttermilk. We were sitting on a fence, keeping our eyes peeled for trouble, while a woman churned, when we heard cannon booming. We did not wait for the butter to come, but ran for camp, with our appetite for the buttermilk entirely gone. We afterward learned that the cannon were celebrating the victory at Shiloh, or that at Island Number 10, I have forgotten which. Here (at Keetsville) our company had three recruits from Arkansas—one from near Hot Springs, and two from near Duvall's Bluff.

Before leaving Cassville, thirty of us were sent to White Rock Prairie—35 miles—in wagons, to move out thirteen Union families. We stayed overnight, but had no trouble with the guerillas with whom the country swarmed. We confiscated teams to help move the Union families to Cassville, their teams and entire possessions having been confiscated the night before. We also brought back to Cassville seven prisoners—four of whom we captured on the way, and three where we spent the night.

On July 1 we broke camp at Cassville and started back for Springfield, Missouri, arriving there on July 3. We remained in Springfield till September, going on numerous scouting expeditions and working on fortifications.

I had charge of forty men for six weeks, working on Fort Number One. Reinforcements came from the north, swelling our forces to about one thousand[24].

---

[24] The regiment, and his company, were now back to full strength. This was a major influx of new recruits.

Newtonia—Marching, Skirmishing, etc.

Leaving Springfield early in September [1862], we marched to Newtonia, where a rebel recruiting camp of several thousand was situated. On the night before we reached Newtonia we cleared ground, and made an appearance of preparing to camp for some time; but, after dark, broke camp and continued our march. We reached Newtonia about daylight, drove rebel pickets before us and followed them in on to a prairie in sight of Newtonia. Finding rebels in line of battle at Newtonia, we opened artillery fire and they retreated to the south, leaving us in possession.

After camping south of Newtonia two days, we were ordered to break camp and march—we knew not where. Though it was raining like Jehu[25], the bugle sounded, and we marched toward Cassville. It rained hard all day, and we went into camp twelve miles from Cassville. Our wagons being behind, we had no rations and tents.

Next morning the wagons came up and we butchered beef, etc., and filled up. [We] Continued our march to Cassville that day, where we stayed a few days, and then

---

[25] Jehu was King of Israel in the 9th century BC. In the Bible, II Kings chapters 9-10 tell the story of how Jehu "drove [his chariot] furiously". Swap is saying that the rain was driving furiously.

marched north on the Springfield road. At a tavern called Three Widows the road forked, the main road going to Springfield and the other to Mt. Vernon. We took the latter as far as Marysville.

During this march several of the boys were tied to the rear of wagons by their thumbs, as a punishment for straggling, foraging without orders, etc., by order of commanding officer, General "Jimmie" Totten[26].

While we were at Marysville, where we stayed several days, the brigade sutler[27] was raided by the boys, who did not like him, and his stores confiscated. To find the guilty parties, the entire division was ordered out, and all quarters were searched; but nothing incriminating was found.

Breaking camp we marched in one day to Ozark, Missouri, 35 miles distant, with "beds on back." All of our company fell out by the way, unable to keep up, except enough to make two stacks of arms—eight—myself among them.

---

[26] Brigadier General James Totten (1818-1871) was a career soldier with a mediocre record. He was dismissed in 1870 for "Disobedience of Orders" and "Neglect of Duty."

[27] A sutler was a civilian who was authorized (licensed) to operate a store on, with or near an army camp, post or fort. Usually operating from a tent or a wagon, they usually supplied items not supplied by the Army, but were wanted by soldiers—everything from tobacco to postage stamps, often with exorbitant markup.

Newtonia—Marching, Skirmishing, etc.

On this 35-mile march we ate our dinner on the battle ground of Wilson's Creek, where General Lyon[28], the "Savior of Missouri," had been killed in July.

This was a severe march. The days were short, and the march was completed "from sun to sun." Some artillery horses died by the way, and also some members of a green regiment. This murderous march was caused by strife and emulation between the cavalry and infantry, and served no real purpose.

We camped at Ozark a few days, then took up our line of march southwest. It rained all day, and the regimen arrived late at night at Camp Halleck, near Dug Spring, where we remained two days and then marched south of Springfield toward Fayetteville, Arkansas, to reinforce General Blunt[29] at Kane Hill, Arkansas.

---

[28] Brigadier General Nathaniel Lyon (1818-1861) was the first Union general to be killed in the Civil War, on July 13, 1861 during the Battle of Wilson's Creek.

[29] Major General James Gilpatrick Blunt (1826-1881) was a physician and abolitionist active in early Republican (party) politics.

Battle of Prairie Grove—Disciplined—
On to Cape Girardeau

After marching about twenty-five miles a day, for two days, we camped at Camp Siegel, two miles south of Keetsville [Missouri]. We received "hurry" orders, and at daylight took up our line of march, arriving at Illinois Creek, ten miles southwest of Fayetteville, the next morning, December 7, 1862, having marched fifty miles in twenty-four hours. Before reaching Illinois Creek we met retreating Missouri calvary, who reported fighting ahead, and said that cavalry had been nearly all captured.

We crossed Illinois Creek, and our artillery took position on the edge of the prairie south of the creek, where we opened fire on the enemy, who was located in the timber, south of the prairie. After silencing the enemy's batteries, our infantry advanced across the prairie, and engaged the enemy in his position. The 17th Iowa and 20th Wisconsin advanced up the hill and drove the enemy from one his batteries, but were greatly outnumbered, and had to retreat, with great slaughter. I saw one company of the 20th Wisconsin carry out twenty men dead from their company.

After these regiments retreated, the 37th Illinois (mine), and the 26th Indiana were ordered up the hill to take their place. After engaging the enemy for a short time we were forced back behind our batteries, which opened on the enemy with terrible effect, and checked his advance.

While retreating down the hill—before this last engagement—I crouched down in a corner of a fence, and busied myself shooting; and my regiment retreated still further, without my observing them. When I became aware that I was left behind, I ran diagonally through the corn field, not to give the Johnnies a straight view of me between the rows; but the bullets rattled merrily in the corn on both sides of me. Before I reached my regiment again, I came across Tom Paine, leaning against a tree pale and trembling, insisting that he was shot, and that the blood was flowing into his boots. It turned out that he had not a scratch, and was plain scared. He afterwards received a medal of honor! [30]

While the artillery was still firing on the enemy in front, we heard the boom of cannon to the west. It was soon rumored that [General] Blunt had come in from that direction to re-enforce us, and attacked the enemy's left flank. Soon after this welcome news, the enemy was seen drifting through the woods towards their right, retreating from Blunt's attack. Our batteries redoubled their fire

---

[30] The list of American Medal of Honor recipients does not include Paine. He must have received a lesser award for valor—but not "The" Medal of Honor, which is our nation's highest honor.

and made it interesting for the Johnnies till dark, when the conflict ceased.

This battle of Prairie Grove resulted in a Union victory: but out of two hundred and fifty men of our regiment who went into battle, seventy-four were lost, in killed and wounded. Lendrick Sproul, a private in Company E, being wounded in the knee, dragged his leg and carried his gun and accoutrements at least half a mile to the rear, going on one knee; "because," he said, "he would be damned if he would leave them for the Johnnies." We found him by a fire, after the battle. He died of gangrene, three weeks later, having refused amputation.

After burying the dead and caring for the wounded, we marched for Van Buren, Arkansas, across the Boston Mountains. We had a slight skirmish with the enemy, who preceded us, but he got away across the river. All we got there was two steamboats of commissary supplies which we destroyed.

After resting a day, we returned to Fayetteville, Arkansas, then went to Huntsville Arkansas. There it came on wet and muddy, with roads almost impassable. The Confederate cavalry general, Marmaduke[31], swung around to the east of us to raid Springfield, our base of supplies. Our infantry and artillery stuck in the mud and could not pursue, though we tried six teams on each gun; so Marmaduke got away. When he arrived at Springfield, he was confronted by the 18th Iowa, convalescents from

---

[31] Confederate Major General John Sappington Marmaduke was a West Point graduate whose father was the 8th governor of Missouri. He later served as the 25th governor of Missouri.

hospital, and inmates of military prison, armed. After a sharp engagement Marmaduke was forced to retire.

From Huntsville we went up on the Springfield road and camped out at roll call, and I was placed on special duty for not being up at roll call. As our penalty we were sent out with a team to get wood for the company. We cut a load of good wood for each tent in the company, then got the worst water elm we could find for the captain's tent. We did not stop to unload, but sneaked into our tents. Captain Smith came out and viewed it with a broad grin, and we heard nothing more about it. (Our captain now was Henry Smith, Captain Rust having resigned on account of ill health.)

From Three Widows we marched to Elkhorn Tavern, and hence to Huntsville, Arkansas. Rebels in force were reported to be here, but all we got out of them was a skirmish. We now took up our line of march for Raleigh, Missouri, camping by the way of Elk River, where we stopped a few days to rest. From here we proceeded to Cave Spring, ten miles south of Raleigh, where we camped several days, following a regular camp routine, drilling, etc.; even indulging in a prize fight, in which Rob Ashley was one of the principals. We had, also, two wrestling matches between our regiment and the 20th Iowa, our man winning in both cases.

About April 1, 1863, we marched to Raleigh, Missouri, and took passage on flat cars (Uncle Sam's coaches) for St. Louis, Missouri. The cars ran so fast we could hardly stick on them. Arriving in St. Louis we entered camp at Camp Jackson, and remained till after the celebration of the battle of Camp Jackson[32], which had occurred two years before. At this celebration a soldier only had to say "I fight mit Siegel[33]" to get well filled with drinkables.

---

[32] Also called the "Camp Jackson Affair" or the "St Louis Riots" of May 10, 1861 in which over 75 civilians, including women and children, were killed.

[33] He is most likely referencing the fatal wounding of Captain Constantin Blandowski of the 3rd Missouri Volunteer Infantry, who died—although often described as "German" or "Dutch" (Deutch), he was ethnically Polish, born on the German side of the frontier.

Girardeu—The Little Drummer

We remained in St. Louis till about the last of April [1863], when our regiment was ordered by steamer to Cape Girardeau, Missouri, which was being besieged by the Confederate general, [John S.] Marmaduke. On out arrival at Cape Girardeau, [the] siege was raised on account of the reinforcement of the garrison. Arrived at Cape Girardeau, we were lined-up; and one Balcomb, who had shown marked ingenuity in getting himself detailed to some other duty than fighting, had difficulty in getting his cartridge into his gun, having, finally, to fall back to the sidewalk where he could punch his ramrod against the fence. Later, in his hearing, someone asked where was Balcomb, and a boy replied that the last time he saw Balcomb he was trying to bite off his cartridge, but had the wrong end in his mouth and was trying to bite off the ball.[34]

We remained at Cape Girardeau till the next night; then marched in pursuit of the enemy. We travelled all night and all the next day and overtook the rearguard just at night. We had expected the forces from Iron Mountain

---

[34] Any veteran will appreciate the humor of this anecdote—every military unit has a Balcomb… or two.

to be in Marmaduke's front by this time, but they had been delayed and the trap was not closed. It was a severe chase from there—about three days—marching and skirmishing to St. Francis River, ninety miles from Cape Girardeau.

Battle of Chalk Bluff[35]

The enemy having crossed the St. Francis and destroyed the bridge before we could get there, we deployed along the river bank and had a sharp engagement, fighting across the river. All who could do so got behind trees. Al Cooley and I got behind the same tree, and shrank ourselves as small as possible, to make it cover us. We were soon ordered to fall back to the foot of the hill, in order to permit the artillery to fire. This battle of Chalk Bluff on the St. Francis River was rather barren of results.

At the battle of Chalk Bluff occurred one of the most pathetic incidents of the way. Little Charlie Eaton, ten years old, was a drummer in Company H, 37th Illinois, of which his father was first lieutenant. Having marched day and night, Charlie slept in his sleeping father's arms, lying in front of, and under, the batteries (fourteen guns) which were firing over us. A percussion shell, striking a tree, exploded and a piece struck Lieutenant Eaton, killing him instantly. Some of the boys took little Charlie

---

[35] May 1-2, 1863, in Clay County, Arkansas. Brigadier General William Vandever unsuccessfully attempted to block Marmaduke from crossing the St. Francis River. Marmaduke "won" but had high casualties, abandoned this second expedition into Missouri.

from his dead father's arms—still sleeping! One of the boys who performed this service for the little drummer boy, told me this part of the story at the Buffalo reunion.

Having chased the enemy across the St. Francis and accomplished all we could at Chalk Bluff, we marched leisurely back to Cape Girardeau. Some three days later we took steamer back to St. Louis, and encamped; and in a few days were ordered to Iron Mountain—this time by rail, in box cars. Here smallpox broke out in the command and the men were all ordered vaccinated.

Siege of Vicksburg—Yazoo City

We stayed here, Iron Mountain, about two weeks; then marched for St. Genivieve, Missouri, a French town which remained neutral and prosperous. Here our division took steamer [south] for Vicksburg, Mississippi. Arriving at Young's Point, opposite Vicksburg, about June 6, 1863, we were welcomed by shots from a battery on the Vicksburg side, three miles distant (not far for guns to "carry" now, but a long way then.) We marched across Young's Point and took steamer to Warrington, Mississippi. Here we landed, marched to vicinity of Vicksburg and took position on the left of the line, thus filling a gap on the extreme left, and all surrounding Vicksburg. We now settled down to siege work: digging pits, planting siege guns, and building forts for our light batteries. All this was night work. We got so close with the pits that we dare not stick out a head by daylight.

Before our arrival an attempt had been made to take the town by assault. Failing in this, the Union tactics, after our arrival, were to starve Vicksburg out. There was, of course, considerable firing from pits in the early morning, at which time the pickets were relieved and went back to quarters. Thirty men, of whom I was one, were detailed on a scout. We filed silently down on the river bottom, and worked our way inside the enemy's lines, where we could see them at work, digging, etc. Had they become aware of our presence, they could easily have cut us off; but the woods were thick, and were able to make our observations unseen.

One of the enemy's guns was called Whistling Dick, because of a whistling noise that its two-foot projectile made in the air. This gun threw its projectile three miles across Young's Point, and fired on the troops and supplies as the transports landed. It was over-charged one day, and exploded, bursting off about three feet off its muzzle and putting Whistling Dick out of commission. During the siege our mortar boats from Young's Point were continually shelling Vicksburg. The shells were exploded by means of a fuse; and we could trace their course by the tail of fire behind them. One of these shells would demolish a building.

Vicksburg surrendered on July 4, 1863, and we entered amid great rejoicing. Captured fireworks were set off and general highjinks were indulged in. Vicksburg had consumed all its food supplies—even to its mules—and 32,000 rations were issued to the besieged immediately upon its surrender.

Grant[36] was in command at Vicksburg. He went around in a slouch hat and common blouse, with no rank straps and inspected the pits. It was currently reported that our division officers went to him and urged him to again assault. He told them they might have guns and

---

[36] General Ulysses Simpson Grant, who later commanded all Union forces and became the 18th American President. His nickname was "Unconditional Surrender" Grant.

ammunition, and assault Vicksburg themselves, but could not have his men. He had enough of that on the 22d of May. He was the ideal soldier of the rank and file.

The fruit of the victory at Vicksburg was the virtual opening of the river (Mississippi) from its source to the gulf. About 300 siege and field guns and forty or fifty thousand stands of small arms and an immense store of ammunition were captured also[37].

I was on duty in the rifle pits the night before the surrender; but on the day of capitulation was down with malarial fever, and didn't care who surrendered.

On the second day after the fall of Vicksburg Hern's division was ordered up Yazoo River, by steamer to Yazoo City, where a considerable rebel force was stationed. They retreated without severe fighting. I was in convalescent camp with many others. Malaria could be cut with a knife—water very bad. We were camped in dog tents, pitched one above the other in places dug from a side hill. The water had a scum on it every morning.[38]

---

[37] These were muskets that had been smuggled past the blockade, and they were *greatly* inferior to the much more accurate (and deadly) rifled musket used by the Union. The rifled musket used the distinctive Minié ball, which had a much longer range, and which on impact with human flesh, flattened out—or worse, splintered into fragments, causing horrific wounds. Swap would have carried a rifled musket.

[38] For hundreds of years it was believed that malaria was due to "mal air", since the disease was associated with swamps. Its cause is the spreading of Plasmodium parasites through mosquito bite. There are modern preventative steps, medicines, and even cures but it continues to be a killer even in the 21st century. The worst forms of malaria cause permanent debilitation or death.

In Louisiana—Morganza Bend—On to Rio Grande—Chumming with the Mexicans

At the end of the week the regiment returned from Yazoo, and I reported for duty. The division took transports to Port Hudson, Louisiana, and remained here several days; [we] then took steamer for New Orleans. We landed at Carlton, three miles above the city, and went into camp. While here [we were a part of] the 13th Army Corps, commanded by General McLearned[39]. We were then reviewed by General Grant.

Shortly afterward our division—then under General Dana[40], General Heron having been transferred—was ordered to Morganza Bend, above Baton Rouge, where the rebel general, Dick Taylor[41], had been intercepting

---

[39] Major General John Alexander McLearned (1812-1900) was a career politician and a subordinate to Grant.

[40] Major General Napoleon Jackson T. Dana (1822-1905) was a career Army officer who served with distinction. He had a successful business career after the war.

[41] Lt. General Richard Taylor (1826-1879) was a planter, politician and historian. He was the son of former US President Zachary Taylor. His plantation home was destroyed during the war.

river transportation. We pushed him back and held the bend. Taylor's forces fell back across Achafaylaya Bayou. Seven miles out from Morganza Bend, some of our troops were surprised and captured, and we were sent in pursuit. We were cooking supper when the bugle sounded "fall in." In five minutes, we were in line on the levee. General Dana said it was the quickest work he had seen in any regiment. We found our dead thrown into a ditch in a barnyard with a little earth thrown over them—leaving corpses more or less exposed. We pursued the enemy, but he got off across the bayou.

Expecting Taylor after us, we made fortifications of the levees, burning all buildings in front in order to give us a clean sweep with our artillery. Taylor failed to materialize, and we could only capture what rebel sheep, molasses, etc., we could find. We were encamped between levee and river. In a short time, we returned to New Orleans and painted the town vermillion whenever we could get passes to go in. Here I saw my first play, attending a performance of J. Wilkes Booth, the assassin of President Lincoln. After this I went to the theater whenever I got a chance.

About the middle of October [1863], we left New Orleans by ocean steamer for Brownsville, Texas. A squall came up, our rudder chain broke, and we drifted with the wind till morning, when we fixed a spar to use as a rudder, and made back for the fleet, overtaking it at night. We then kept on our course till we reached the mouth of Brazos Bay. The water was so slow on the bar that our boat, the Peabody, was forced to lighten

In Louisiana—Morganza Bend—On to Rio Grande...

by throwing overboard the artillery horses. Only one of these poor brute victims of a man's war succeeded in swimming ashore. Still we could not cross, and were transferred to a lighter boat, but the hour being late, we could not cross the bar that night. This latter boat had been used to transport horses and mules; and the deck, on which we had to sleep, was six inches deep with filth. Next morning, we crossed and were landed at Brazos Island.

We were ten days on this voyage, and I was sick as a dog all the time, but unable to vomit. We were a happy set of boys to be on land again, even if the land was only a sand island. During our two days stay here we only had a pint of water a day each. This was drawn from an ocean steamer. For recreation, at low tide we went and pried out small oysters from large neglected beds.

On the morning of the third day, we were ordered to march for Brownsville, Texas. We soon came to an arm at the bay, which extends from bay to gulf and forms the island of Brazos de Santiago. Just at nightfall we reached the Rio Grande—the first fresh water since leaving New Orleans. The boys had to take fearful and wonderful positions to drink from the river, and quench a thirst three days old.

The hardest rain I ever saw fell while we were encamped that night. I was on guard, and lucky to be so, as nobody could lie down anyhow. In the morning we proceed toward Brownsville, crossing the Mexican battlefields of Palto Alto and Reseca de la Palma. Arrived at Brownsville, we marched through the town and camped on the banks of the Rio Grande, opposite Metamoras, Mexico.

At this time Emperor Maximillian[42] was in Mexico trying to subdue the Mexicans and establish an empire, assisted by the French. The Imperialists were now in possession of Metamoras, but soon after our arrival at Brownsville, the Mexican General, Cortena[43], attacked them and drove them out, taking possession of Metamoras himself. We found it interesting to look on war from the outside. There was a big racket all night— roosters crowing, dog barking and policeman shouting all over the city.

The Rio was not so "Grande" as its name here, and we could almost skip a stone across it. It was hardly navigable for boats drawing 8 inches of water[44], so we were close to the fight.

After the Mexicans (the Liberals) got possession their officers and ours exchanged courtesies, crossing back and forth to view parades, etc. The Mexican officers with true "greaser" love of finery, were gorgeously appareled; wearing hats worth $75.00 and $100.00, and

---

[42] Maximilian (1832-1867) was an Austrian archduke who created a "Second Mexican Empire" from 1864 until executed in 1867. His name will re-appear towards the end of this narrative.

[43] Juan Cortina (not "Cortena") (1824-1870) was a Mexican rancher, politician, military leader, outlaw and folk hero. He is best known for the First and Second Cortina Wars in 1859 & 1861.

[44] This is most likely true. In many places the river is only inches deep, especially during dry seasons.

with gold and silver lace much in evidence about their uniforms.

I was in Metamoras twice. On one occasion I visited a fashionable bazaar, a gambling place, where I saw bushels of gold and silver staked—principally at roulette. The croupiers etc., were most gorgeously arrayed and were mostly Spaniards. The Mexicans were very friendly and were lavish in praise of the American "Soldado Mucho[45]." One American, however, was killed in a gambling place. His bowels were taken out and replaced by sand, and the body was sunk in the river.

The water used in Brownsville was delivered by carriers, in barrels with a rope attached at each end and an axle in the middle. The carrier would roll his barrel into the river, fill it; and then, taking his rope, drag it through the streets. I saw Mexicans delivering wood in Brownsville—practically a Mexican town, then—with a drove of burros. Half a cord was strapped on each one, and a man—also mounted on a burro—rode behind.

Milk, butter and cheese were produced from flocks of goats, which were kept in great numbers and ranged in the chaparral near the town. A Mexican woman milked a goat by catching and holding one of its hind legs between her knees. We could not at first eat much of the Mexican food in restaurants, it was so hot with red pepper. Meat was preserved by drying it in the sun.

---

[45] Literally "soldier a lot". It was a compliment.

Fun in Camp—Free State Festivities

About December 1 [1863], our regiment was ordered up to Ringbold [Ringgold] Barracks[46]—seven companies by steamer, and three in army wagons by land—to secure military stores that had been captured from the rebels, but low water prevented us from approaching nearer than thirty miles. We stopped a few days—we in the boats—till the land expedition secured the supplies and returned. On starting from Brownsville, we had taken ten days' rations, but were gone twenty-one days. We lived, largely, on beef of confiscated cattle. This beef was often without salt, and were glad to get back to our old camp at Brownsville.

On the return trip, while encamped on shore one evening, three men went after beef, one armed with a gun, one with a hatchet and one with a knife. A steer was shot and fell. The "knife man" ran to cut his throat, but the steer jumped up, and the "hatchet man"—one Keech—caught him by the tail. After making Keech's heels fly for

---

[46] Fort Ringgold was the southernmost installation of the western forts constructed at the end of the Mexican War in 1848, and was an active US Army post for nearly a century. It played an important role in the Cortina Wars described by Swap. The US Army disposed of the fort in 1944.

a little way the steer got away, first peppering Keech well with mud and filth, in the face and front of his clothes. This was a good joke for the boys.

On the last night of the return trip, within six miles of Brownsville—by land—orders were issued not to kill any cattle, and a guard was placed to prevent anyone from landing with guns, but when the boats touched the boys swarmed ashore, with guns and without. Those with guns went in pursuit of cattle, being hungry and having had their request to be allowed to march on to Brownsville refused. Those who were unarmed assembled on the bank and threw stones at the officers' cabin. As soon as possible, the commanding officer went ashore and gave orders permitting them to kill all the beef they wanted.

Opposite our camp the river took a short bend; the boat could hardly turn and had to be brought up with a chug against the bank before it could turn. We arrived at Brownsville about four o'clock of the next day, and were glad to get back to hard tack and coffee.

During our absence up river, Abe Puterbaugh and Harry Smith, chums, being short of a tent, conceived the idea of confiscating one. After night they went to the camp of the 91st Illinois and finding an "A" tent that suited them, silently pulled the pegs, and lifted the tent from four sleepers, who awoke in the morning to find themselves roofed only by the sky. Before going to sleep under their newly acquired tent, the boys covered the number and letters on it with old canvas, and were undiscovered by the search party that was sent out next day.

FUN IN CAMP—FREE STATE FESTIVITIES

Puterbaugh was a reliable thief. Near Pea Ridge the captain said to him "Abe, there's a nice lot of pigs out there in the brush—orders are not to shoot any." Of course, the captain had pork for supper.

We stayed at Brownsville till February 10th [1864]. The regiment was offered thirty days furlough and additional bounty if they would re-enlist "for three years or during the war." Enough of the men re-enlisted—myself among them—to veteranize the regiment. On the 10th of February, 1864, we marched to Point Isabel, on Brazos Bay, were placed aboard [a] steamer and went to New Orleans, forty-eight hours' run. The gulf was smooth as glass, but with a dead swell that brought up everything I had ever eaten in my life, in fifteen minutes.

In the New Orleans we were quartered in Factor's Cotton Press on Tchoupitulas Street. Here we remained long enough to participate in the festivities attending the inauguration of Governor Hand [47], Louisiana's first "free state" governor. Our part was to guard a passage from the State House to La Fayette Square, to where the ceremony took place[48].

There was said to be five hundred instruments in the brass band, playing national airs. Artillery and infantry, firing by file, platoon and company, contributed to the

---

[47] Michael Hahn (1830-1886) was an attorney, publisher, planter, and former US Congressman. He was our nation's first ethnically Jewish and first German-born governor.

[48] Since Hahn was a "Union" governor, and tempers remained hot in Louisiana (who was in rebellion), a Union Army guard for his inauguration would very much be in order.

patriotic din. The artillery was fired by the band leader, by means of electricity. After the inauguration it was impossible to get out of the square. Our regiment had to press the crowd slowly back at the point of the bayonet. One negro cab driver had actually to be prodded to make him move on. At night we attended the magnificent fireworks with balls in our guns (which had been filled with blank cartridges during the day) for fear of riot, but no trouble occurred.

Soon after this we took the steamer Hope. St. Louis was only 1,200 miles distant, but we had to "Hope" for ten days before we reached it.

LORETTA CATHERINE DE WOLF
Daughter of William Bills and Catherine Harrington De Wolf
Born July 25th, 1840

The Daguerreotype of his fiancée, which was the
original of this picture, was carried by A. L. Swap, from the time
of his furlough in 1864, through the remaining years of service

Furlough—Forgotten Etiquette—
Back South

We landed at East St. Louis [Illinois], and, next day went by rail to Chicago. Here a reception with a fine banquet was tendered us at the "Soldiers' Rest." A nice young lady passed me a plate of meat; and having almost forgotten the use of knives and forks, I took apiece with my fingers—much to my chagrin when I caught myself.

On March 24 [1864] we received our furloughs for thirty days. I first visited my parents in La Salle County, Illinois, then my brother in Wisconsin. After this I went to [my] boyhood's home in Pennsylvania, accompanied by my sister, Prudence. I went back to La Salle County, stayed there a short time, and returned to Chicago on April 24. On my way from my parent's place in Mendota, where I took the train, I chilled during the entire nine-mile drive. I had never been free from malaria, in some form, since my attack of malarial fever at Vicksburg.

We left Chicago on the 25th, packed into box cars, and had an awful night—freezing weather and no ventilation. The boys kicked holes in the sides of the cars. I ached and "fevered" all night. Reaching Cairo in the forenoon of the 26th, we lay around the levees and froze till night, then took steamer for Memphis, Tennessee. We were on the upper deck, exposed to a cold west wind, which froze me some more.

Landing in due time at Memphis, our regiment was stopped there to re-enforce the Memphis forces against General Forrest [49], who was operating in that vicinity. It was a rear chase to Corinth, Mississippi, then the regiment returned to Memphis, leaving me in convalescent camp. While here I found my brother, Bert, of the 7th Illinois Cavalry, and we had a good visit together.

The regiment was gone perhaps a week, and upon its return, took steamer for Nachez, Mississippi, where we were ordered up [the] Red River, to guard supply boats enroute to Bank's army up the river. At the mouth of Red River we learned that Banks was on the retreat, so we proceeded to Old River, where we assisted in the building of a bridge for the passage of Bank's retreating army [50]. Thirteen steamboats were anchored in line, their bows upstream. Gangplanks extending from bow to bow formed the bridge. We could hear the firing of big guns as Banks retreated toward the river.

---

[49] Lt. General Nathan Bedford Forrest (1821-1877) was a former planter, slave trader and real estate broker. He was later the first Grand Wizard of the Ku Klux Klan.

[50] Major General Nathaniel Prentice Banks (1816-1894) was a former millworker and career politician from Massachusetts and the former Speaker of the House. While a successful politician, he performed poorly as a general.

Furlough—Forgotten Etiquette—Back South

We now marched for Morganza Bend, and encamped above the Bend. Here I received my first and only reprimand—or near-reprimand. Upon the sounding of an orderly call, Orderly Sergeant McCord was missing, and I was obliged to take his place on the detailing of guards. This duty being an unexpected one to one, and, being conscientious on the selection of men who had not last served, it took me some time, so that I was the last orderly to report with the guard. The Colonel said "Sergeant Swap, report at my tent after guard mount." This I did and he rebuked me for the delay.

When I could get in a word, I told him that it was not my duty to detail guards that day, and that I was doing McCord's work. He said "Tell Sergeant McCord to report to me." This I did most cheerfully, and after this interview McCord was never again missing at orderly call. I felt the rebuke to be unjust and thought it would have been gentlemanly in the Colonel to recall it, after learning the facts, so I was in the mood to enjoy the story on him which was told me by Sergeant Mauser. Being called to the Colonel's tent, the latter said to him, "Sergeant Mauser, when you go into a neighbor's house what is the first thing you do?" Colonel B.," was the reply, "if the neighbor has manners enough to ask me to sit down, I take off my hat." "Sit down, Sergeant Mauser, sit down," replied the Colonel.

We remained in camp above Morganza Bend about two weeks. Fishing was our main recreation here. We caught some big catfish and some white bass. One man caught a catfish weighing 60 pounds.

I think our next move was to take transports to White River Landing, Arkansas. From here we went up White River to St. Charles, Arkansas, where we built fortifications to repel attack by rebels supposed to be in that vicinity. We were not attacked; and, the rebels retiring, we proceeded to Duvall's Bluff, where we went to Winter quarters, remaining there till the last of February, 1865. We built log shanties here, and rived our own "shakes" to roof them; but only occupied them some six weeks.

During this time I went with an Arkansas man to Little Rock to get a large camp kettle for a stove, also a tin stove pipe, and a large window light. The kettle, with a hole cut for pipe, and one for draft, made a fine stove. We got back to Duvall's Bluff after dark; and, carrying the window pane from the train to our hut, I fell down and broke it.

This companion of mine—John Donovan—when he enlisted, left a fifteen-year-old brother at home, twelve miles from Duvall's Bluff. While we were encamped there he wished to go after his brother, but the country being full of guerillas, he could not get a pass. Twelve of us told Captain Day (Captain Smith had died of smallpox while on veteran furlough) that we were going anyhow. He replied that we took our own risks. At night we went up river on a skiff, then walked out to where the boy was with a cousin—a guerilla. We lay quiet that night with a Union man, and returned to camp next day. Donovan sent the boy north, out of that dangerous country, with a returning comrade. He—Donovan—was killed here soon after the war by bushwhackers.

Furlough—Forgotten Etiquette—Back South

Leaving Duvall's Bluff, we took transports to ten miles above New Orleans, and camped here in the mud, idle, for six weeks. About the middle of March, we took steamers for Pensacola, Florida, landing in the harbor across the bay from Fort Jackson, one of several old Spanish forts in this locality. In a few days we marched for Pensacola, and, two days later, for Blakely, Alabama.

Siege and Assault of Blakely, Alabama—Lee's Surrender—Hunting Alligators—Another Furlough

We arrived in the rear of Fort Blakely on April 1, 1865. On this march we boiled corn which we scratched up out of the sand after mules had been fed.

Our march was delayed by inadequate transportation. Wagons sank into the sand to the hub, after rain. At Blakely, our supplies coming up from the bay we filled up. We were now a part of Second Division, 13th Corps, command by General Fred Steele [51].

On our arrival in the rear of Ft. Blakely, we had no entrenching tools for four days. We drove in the enemy's skirmishers, and confined then to their rifle pits in front of their works. Entrenching tools came from below, and we began to dig rifle pits, and to advance on the enemy, throwing up breastworks for our batteries.

My bunk mate, Puterbaugh, was on picket duty one day, and I took him a warm dinner. They told me about the surgeon having come out to them, and wishing he

---

[51] Major General Frederick Steele (1819-1868) was a highly effective career US Army officer, who in addition to his Civil War exploits had been decorated for bravery during the Mexican War.

could take a shot. Puterbaugh offered his gun, saying it was not loaded. He then put in load on top of the one already in it. The surgeon shot and kicked himself back against the wall of the pit. I stood against the pit, chuckling over the joke on the surgeon, not noticing that my head was above the bank, when a bullet struck the earth and threw it all over me, taking the laugh all out of me.

We settled down to besieging Ft. Blakely, advancing our works, etc., till the evening of the 9th of April [1865]. It was rumored that the enemy's works were to be assaulted that afternoon.

About 5 o'clock [pm], assembly was sounded and the troops marched front and occupied a reserve rifle pit. The men in our advance were ordered forward to drive the enemy from his advance pits. This was done. A strong skirmish line was sent forward with orders to advance and command the embrasures of the enemy's siege guns. The headquarters bugle sounded the charge, which was taken up by division brigade buglers and the regimental buglers, and the entire line moved forward to the assault. Our main pit being four feet deep with earth thrown up in front, it was difficult for small men to get out. The captain ordered Ike Rose and me to stay in the pit and help the little fellows out. This done we followed up, charging on our own hook, and entering the enemy's works with the rest of the command. We captured the whole line of works with four thousand prisoners and forty heavy guns, etc. This opened the way to Mobile [Alabama].

SIEGE AND ASSAULT OF BLAKELY, ALA.—LEE'S SURRENDER...

After entering, a comrade said to me, "I thought you were dead. I saw you fall outside the enemy's works." I had been jumping from one to another of the legs that had been felled, with sharpened stubs left sticking up, to impeded our advance, and had jumped short and fallen. On all open ground between the enemy's time and ours, at Blakely, they had planted torpedoes to blow us up. The wire extended from them which being stepped upon or against exploded them. These torpedoes did no material damage at the time of the charge, but a number of early stragglers returning to camp after it, were blown up by them; and when we returned in a body, guards had been placed at these torpedo beds to warn us off.

For two days after this, rebel prisoners were employed, under guard, to remove the torpedoes. Those that they could dig out they exploded with a stick, lying back away from them to avoid the explosion.

On the third day after this engagement we took steamers from Mobile, where we remained one day, then took steamers [up the Alabama River] for Montgomery, Alabama. This was under General Steele.

We expected to reach Selma before General Wilson[52] left; but he, being on a raid, had to leave, having captured Selma with its arsenals, great store of small arms and nearly all the opposing troops, and destroyed much rebel property.

---

[52] Major General James H. Wilson (1837-1925) was a topographical engineer and the leader of "Wilson's Raid", an April 1865 Union calvary raid into Alabama and Georgia.

When we were a few miles below Cahaba prison pen, guerillas rode up on the river bluff and fired on our boat—Steele's headquarters—killing one man and wounding two others. We afterward burned the fine plantation home of the Captain of this guerila band.

It was rumored before we started on this trip that [Confederate General Robert E.] Lee had surrendered, and on the way up [river], before reaching Selma, we met a Union officer and two Confederates coming down with small boats. They brought definite news of Lee's surrender. We touched at Cahaba, and found that the surrender of Lee had caused the release of all our prisoners except one sick man, whom we took on our boat.

Our next stop was at Selma, where we stayed two days, and then proceeded by steamer to Montgomery, Alabama. Here I visited the capitol where Jeff Davis was inaugurated as President of the Southern Confederacy[53]. We now returned to Selma, where we remained a few days. While here a number of Lee's army returned home after the surrender, asked citizens of Selma for food, which was refused them. Our boys took them in and filled them up[54].

We returned [downriver] to Mobile and went into regular camp three miles above the city. While here "Dick" Taylor surrendered in the interior of Mississippi.

---

[53] Montgomery, Alabama was the first capital of the Confederacy; the capital was moved to Richmond shortly after Virginia succeeded from the Union.

[54] This is an interesting detail- was there a shortage of civilian food in Selma which caused this, or ill feelings towards their soldiers?

Siege and Assault of Blakely, Ala.—Lee's Surrender...

His supplies of ammunition were shipped by rail to Mobile, and stored in a warehouse near the depot. By some accident (or otherwise) this ammunition was fired and caused a tremendous explosion, razing four brick blocks to the ground. At Mobile I paid $1.75 in greenbacks for a dozen eggs, for a sick comrade. This was a highwater mark for [the price of] eggs.

After receiving our pay at Mobile, our regiment moved camp to within city limits, where we did provost duty till last of June [1865], when we were ordered by ocean steamer to Galveston, Texas. We landed here about July 1 and spent Fourth of July, 1865, in Galveston.

After a few days we were ordered, again by ocean steamer, to Sabine City [Texas], where we were gnawed by mosquitoes for about a week. We hunted alligators for two days, and killed a lot of them. On the second day we saw dead ones floating that we had killed the first day.

We now took steamer for Beaumont, Texas, on the Sabine River, and proceeded by rail to Houston. From Houston our regiment was scattered by companies to different Texas points. Five companies, including mine, went to Columbus, on the Colorado River. Our duties here—dress parade in the evening, etc. —were very light. Sweet potatoes being plentiful here, with no one to cut off commissary supplies, we lived high. While here, on this low ground, I had a renewed attack of malarial fever, having had fever, at intervals, ever since the siege of Vicksburg. I also had a troublesome asthmatic cough[55],

---

[55] As noted by De Wolf in her Introduction, Swap carried this asthma with him the rest of his life.

and the captain asked me one day if I wanted a furlough. I said "yes," and shortly received a thirty a day furlough.

I went to Galveston by rail and took ocean steamer to New Orleans, and river boat to Cairo. From here I went by rail to Mendota, Illinois, where I stayed a few days, with my parents. After which I returned to my early home in Pennsylvania and visited my uncle, Jacob Swap. I returned to Cairo and reported at the end of my furlough.

Falling in with two comrades at Cairo, we took river steamer to New Orleans, and kept together till we rejoined our regiment. From New Orleans we took ocean steamer to Galveston, and reported for transportation to Houston, where five companies of our regiment were stationed. It was some two weeks before we received transportation; and we had been absent about two months when we at last rejoined our regiment.

We were camped on Buffalo Bayou, and had no duties except guarding prisoners and commissaries' and quartermasters' stores, etc., and I went swimming every month during the winter. There being no visible reason why we should be kept in the service, we repeatedly petitioned the government of Illinois to intercede, and obtain our discharge, but we were held here till May [1866], when we were mustered out.

We now learned that the disturbance in Mexico had been the cause of our being kept down that way so long; but now, Maximillian having been executed and the trouble ended, we were, at last, permitted to go home.

It seemed unfair for us, who had served so long, to have this added service required of us, but it now transpired that it was because we were veterans that we were wanted for this purpose.

Mustered Out—Final Tragedies— Wedding Bells

We were mustered out on May 15, 1866. About thirty days before, there were seven desertions from our company. Two of the deserters had been through the entire war and had been good soldiers; perhaps the other were, also.

While we were in camp at Galveston, thirty-four men from the 67th Illinois and the 76th Illinois were transferred to our company, Company E, 37th Illinois Infantry[56]. Most of them had served less than two years, and eight had been court-martialed for desertion three years before. Sentence of court-martial had never been received, so they were still under arrest.

On May 15, the day we were mustered out, we took transportation on steamers for Galveston, Texas. Going down Buffalo Bayou, the limbs of trees scraped our boats on both sides, and we could only turn around by backing some distance down the bay.

---

[56] Sergeant Albert Swap's unit, the 37th Illinois Infantry Regiment were also known during the war as "Fremont's Rifles" and/or the "Illinois Greyhounds". From the amount of wartime service they saw and the hard marches conducted early in the conflict in Missouri and Arkansas—both names were appropriate.

Two chums in Company D, having celebrated too much, one of them got up in his sleep and walked off the upper deck in front of the side wheel. His bunkmate rushed down to the lower deck and jumped off, also in front of the wheel. The boat was stopped and search was made, but of course, they were not found. Both were good soldiers and this tragic event saddened the homeward voyage of the boys.

When we reached Galveston, we took ocean steamer for New Orleans, and gladly bade good-bye to Texas. At New Orleans we took river steamboat for Cairo, Illinois, in "God's Country."

At Springfield, Illinois, on May 30, 1866, we received our final discharge and back pay to May 15th, when our discharges were dated[57]. On the day when we received our discharge, I was due to shake, having done so the day but one before[58]. I went to the hospital steward and got our ounces of whiskey and seven army doses of quinine, all of which I took before noon, and have never had an ague chill since.

Before taking train for home, I went to a barber shop, and indulged in a shave, a haircut and a bath; shed my old army clothes on the floor, dressed in a new suit, and

---

[57] As noted previously, Swap was inducted into the regiment at its 1861 formation and was discharged at its 1866 end.

[58] Attacks of malaria typically come in waves. He's stating that two days before his discharge he had an attack, and that based on past experience he was expecting another malarial attack on his discharge day. He notes that the whiskey and quinine, all taken before noon on discharge day, effected his cure.

came out a civilian. I greatly regret that I left my sergeant's roll call in the pocket of the discarded uniform. Money would not buy it if I had it now.

I made a visit to my parents in Illinois and one to my brother Frank in Wisconsin, and then returned to my old home in Pennsylvania.

During my first three years' service, William B. De Wolf, my Uncle Jacob's nearest neighbor, an ardent Unionist, made his daughters, Loretta and Mollie write to me, perhaps to other soldiers also, to help to cheer and encourage us, and we corresponded till the close of the war.

Loretta De Wolf and I were married on September 18, 1866, and "lived happy ever after."

Principal Battles and Skirmishes in which the Thirty-Seventh Illinois Infantry Took Part

Springfield, Missouri............................ February 12, 1862
Sugar Creek, Arkansas .... February 17, 1862
Pea Ridge, Arkansas.......................... March 6, 7, 8, 1862
King's River, Missouri .... May 13, 1862
Neosho, Missouri .... June 1, 1862
Newtonia, Missouri................................ October 4, 1862
Fayetteville, Arkansas .... October 28, 1862
Prairie Grove, Arkansas .... December 7, 1862
Cape Girardeau, Missouri .... April 26, 1863
Chalk Bluff, Missouri................................. May 2, 1863
Vicksburg, Mississippi .... July 13, 1863
Morganza, Louisiana........................ September 29, 1863
Atchafaylaya, Louisiana .... May 31, 1864
Blakely, Alabama .... April 2, 9, 1865

CHILDREN OF A. L. AND LORETTA SWAP

Clara Idelle, (Mrs. Emory Perkins); Alma Estella, (Mrs. Erastus Jay Wolf); Loretta Kate, (Mrs. Fred Swap); Rachel Matilda, (Mrs. Ralph II, Griffey); Maude Melvina, (Mrs. Alva Cheney); Frank La Fayette, (married Eva Mallory.)

MEMORIAL VERSES

IZORA DE WOLF

WRITTEN FOR MEMORIAL SERVICES AT
THE NATIONAL CEMETERY
SEVEN PINES, VA.

Under The Pines
MAY 30, 1909

Under the pines they lie, the valiant band,
    Wide-gathered to the nation's honored grave;
Upon the blood-washed bosom of the land
    They drained their eager loyal hearts to save.

Sevenfold the seven pines have grown since then—
    That distant day adown the path of years,
When battle-cloud enshrouded this fair plain,
    And battle-thunder smote on shuddering ears.

When up the highway— steel girt now and flanked
    By smiling homes and peace-tilled fields of grain—
McClellan's serried thousands poured their ranks,
    And Casey flung him on the foe amain.

Deadly the conflict. Terrible the strife.
    Charge and recoil, recoil and charge again;
While the fierce struggle for a nation's life
    Thundered to heaven and shook the verdant plain.

A. L. Swap in The Civil War

Nor fire nor flood may hinder. Summer hastes
    To bridge the sullen Chickahominy;
Butler's dark legions lie in winnowed heaps;
    Winning in death their longed-for liberty.

But futile were the effort to record
    The list of heroes where, heroic all,
A hundred thousand patriots drew the sword
    That their loved Union stand though they should fall.

And it did stand. Praised be the God Who holds
    The nations in the hollow of His hand!
Our starry banner, cleansed in every fold,
    Floats proudly o'er an undivided land.

Across the bright Potomac's storied flood
    The smiling South extends her gracious hand
To clasp her sister of the Northern blood—
    Thus, reunited, may they ever stand!

'Twas long ago. Sevenfold the seven pines
    Since that far day bitter strife and stress,
And the magnolia of soft Southern climes
    Sighs forth its perfume where our heroes rest.

So sleep, beloved. 'Neath Northern skies today
    Unnumbered reverent thousands gather now,
And haste with loving loyal hands to lay
    The wreath of victory where the brave lie low.

Under The Pines

Ye lie apart. No mourning kindred come
    To water with their tears your fragrant bed.
Only a band of comrades far from home
    Strew flowers above each lovely, pillowed head.

And some—ah generous! —of your ancient foes
    Save a few blossoms from their comrades' graves,
And, valor honoring valor, come to strew
    Peace tokens where the flag above ye waves.

Sleep! 'Neath the pines and the magnolia flowers,
    Sleep on. Our loyal hearts shall ne'er forget.
Yours was the conflict: the proud privilege ours
    To show a grateful land remembers yet.

Fifty Years

MAY 30, 1911

'Tis fifty years; the blood and tears,
    The terror and the woe,
Wild war's alarms, the call to arms;
    'Twas fifty years ago.

When Sumter fell; when shot and shell
    Assailed the nation's guard,
Patriots awoke, and Valor spoke,
    And Loyalty kept ward.

Then o'er the land, uprose a band
    Of stalwart men and brave;
And marched away in war's array,
    To rescue and to save.

Bright youth was there, with eager air,
    And manhood stern and strong,
When forth they went with high intent
    To battle with the wrong.

A. L. Swap in The Civil War

Through blinding tears, mid anguished fears
    Sad woman watched, alone;
Fond mothers prayed, and true wives stayed
    To guard and keep the home.

Four fearful years of blood and tears
    The battle cloud hung o'er
The darkened land: on every hand
    Wild raged a brother's war.

In prison pen, 'mid swamp and fen,
    By bayou and by bay,
In thicket dense, foul Pestilence
    Stalked forth and claimed its prey.

The cannon roared; the unsheathed sword
    Flashed and bit deep, and all
The streams ran red: the sky overhead
    Hung like a funeral pall.

But not in vain the leaden rain,
    The spilled heroic blood;
The patriot's God gave rich reward:
    Firm fixed the Union stood.

* * * *

Fifty Years

'Tis fifty years. The battle scars
    That marred Columbia's breast
Kind time hath healed. The book is sealed:
    The nation is at rest.

Our gallant foe of long ago
    Today our brother stands.
Each honors each. O'er the closed breach
    The Blue and Gray clasp hands.

But let us still remember well
    Where through long years and slow,
Dreamless and still they lie, who fell,
    Some fifty years ago.

Comrades of old, true hearts of gold,
    Together let us stand
With heads low bent, all reverent,
    Upon this holy land,

And laurels lay, this sacred day,
    Above the verdant bed,
Where sleep these brave, who died to save
    Their land; our deathless dead.

A Memorial Day Reminiscence
MAY 30, 1912

Comrade, your hand! it's good to see your face
    A year has passed since last we met, you know.
How swift they fly! they seem to fairly race—
    The years that used to be so long and slow.

Why don't we visit oftener? We could talk
    A week, and not say half that's in our hearts.
We're early; let's sit down here in the shade
    And rest a while, before the service starts.

For I can't march today: that stiffened leg
    I brought from Bull Run as a souvenir,
Is not much better than a wooden peg:
    It never bothered as it has this year.

The weather, may be: and you're coughing, too;
    Your asthma worse? I wish you'd try a change
Of climate—but I'd miss you: for you see
    I know you're there, though out of talk-shot range.

A. L. Swap in The Civil War

Hark to that mock bird! where he sits and sings,
    Up in the top of you, magnolia tree.
And smell the roses: they are sweeter here
    Than anywhere on earth, it seems to me.

Ah, comrade! scent of flowers and song bird
    Seem strange to-day. I'm thinking, when we stood
Upon the field out yonder, how we heard
    The battle-thunder: smelled the reek of blood.

John stood beside me—brother John, my twin,
    Shoulder to shoulder, all that fierce-fought day.
I see him now: blue-eyed and boyish-slim.
    At night, beside me on the field he lay.

The ambulance had missed us: but the Night
    We pitying dews above each burning wound.
The smoked-cloud lifted; and, serene and bright,
    From the high heaven the eternal stars looked down.

I've told you often My own wound was slight;
    But John—I held his head upon my arm:
At last he wandered: "Mother dear, good-night!"
    He softly murmured; kissed me, and was gone.

No comrade, I'm not grieving: his young life
    Upon his country's altar he laid down:
A priceless offering! shall I grudge the gift?
    Look yonder, where that tall tree stands alone.

A Memorial Day Reminiscence

The sunlight sifting through its branches: there
    He lies, my brother. See these roses red?
When "Taps" has sounded I shall place them there.
    But no—I'll lay them 'neath the flag instead.

He would have wished it. Hark! the bugle call.
    The boys are coming—let us get in line.
Who says we're crippled, ill or old, today?
    See where they're marching—just beyond that pine.

The boys: the Boy's! God bless them! here they come.
    Let's hurry on, and meet them on the way:
The faithful remnant of our gallant band.
    God, keep them all till next Memorial Day!

The Rusted Bayonet

MAY 30, 1914—WAR WITH MEXICO THREATHENED

John came in from the fields today,
    Cheeks aflame and eyes alight,
And laid in my lap a rusted blade;
    "Mother, I bring you a gift tonight.

I plowed it up in the field just now,
    Down the brook, where the willows grow;
Don't you remember, mother, dear,
    Where I found the bullets a year ago?

Broken and eaten deep with rust,
    Half its width all crumbled away—
None may read 'neath its cankered crust
    Whether 'twas carried by Blue or Gray?

Still, my mother, it speaks to me
    Out of the tragic long ago,
And tells its tale of heroic deeds.
    Mother, oh mother! it moves me so.

A. L. Swap in The Civil War

Can you not hear it, the bugle call?
    Can you not see their banners wave?
Do you catch the glint of their burnished steel
    As they march to glory or the grave?

'Twas a man's hand wielded this bayonet:
    'Twas a hero's heart 'neath the Blue or the Gray.
Honor called, and the soldier went,
    Loyal and brave, to the deadly fray.

Does he tell the tale to his grandson now?
    Does he sleep in peace in a hero's grave?
What matter? His country called to him,
    And all his manhood he freely gave.

Mother, I would that this blade were mine,
    Burnished and bright as of long ago;
That my country's call I might answer, too,
    And forth to the battles' glory go."

* * * *

The rusted bayonet lay in my lap,
    Broken and brittle with time's decay;
But it stabbed me deep in my mother-heart,
    And, trembling, I weep the night away.

The Rusted Bayonet

Ah, for the thrilling bugle call!
    My ears hear a dirge so sad and slow.
Ah, for the waving banners gay!
    My eyes see the mourner's robe of woe.

To my shuddering sight, the gleaming steel
    Drips with a life-tide read and warm;
And, stark and still on a fierce-fought field,
    I can see a well-loved boyish form.

God, pity us mothers! and turn aside
    The tide of war from our own dear land.
Let not Thy lightnings forge blades of steel
    To place in our son's young, eager hands.

Speak to Thy nations and still their wrath,
    And bid their warrings forever cease.
Grant Thou, Thy people o'er all the earth,
    The priceless boon of a world-wide peace.

About the Second Edition Editor

Ross Statham has a strong interest in American military history, having ancestors who fought on both sides of the Civil War. Ross has studied and hiked many of the major and minor battlefields of the Civil War, having lived in Texas, Louisiana, Alabama, Virginia & Georgia.

His ancestors were among the (colony of) Virginia's earliest settlers and include a signer of *The Virginia Declaration of Rights*, a document that was an important precursor to the American Declaration of Independence shortly thereafter.

He is married to Audrey Ring Statham, whose maternal grandmother was Andrew Swap's granddaughter Alice Swap Hathaway. Audrey seeks to keep Ross on the straight and narrow at all times—with mixed success.

Both Ross and Audrey are US Army veterans, have four children, seven grandchildren and reside in the Florida panhandle with a 10-pound daschund. His hobbies include Bible study, history and cycling.

www.ingramcontent.com/pod-product-compliance
Lightning Source LLC
Chambersburg PA
CBHW070940080526
44589CB00013B/1586